COUNTRY-TUNED HARMONICA

An Illustrated Guide for Melodies & Improvisations

Phil Duncan

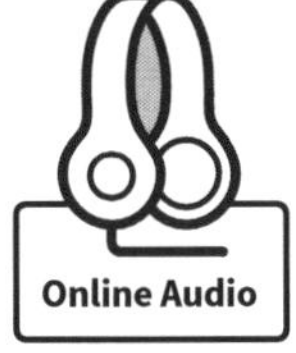

To access the online recording go to:
WWW.MELBAY.COM/30949MEB

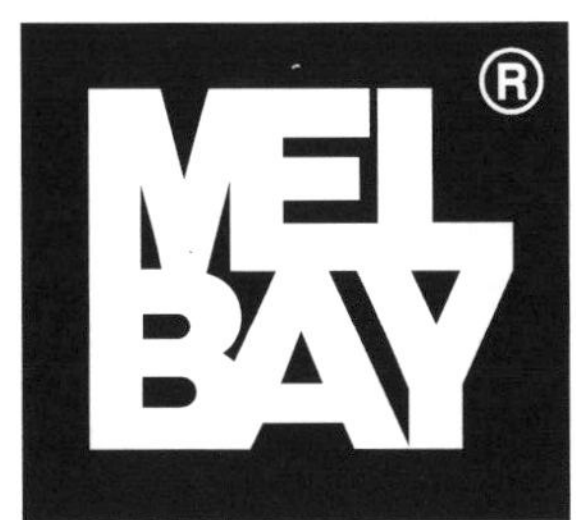

WWW.MELBAY.COM

Table of Contents

****

Alphabetical Listing of Songs

COUNTRY-TUNED HARMONICA
An Illustrated Guide for Melodies and Improvisation

INTRODUCTION

The difference between a standard 10-hole diatonic harmonica and a country-tuned harmonica is the 5th hole of the standard Richter-tuned harmonica draw reed (inhale) is tuned ½ step higher, f to f♯ by thinning the end of the reed. This tuning change creates a major scale, creating an arrangement of whole and half steps, from hole 2 draw to hole 6 Blow; now it is possible to play a complete cross-harp G major scale on the harmonica.

The C harp (cross-harp for G) from hole 2 to 6, raises the 7th pitch to create a G scale:

[2 draw G, 3 *draw-bend a*, 3 draw b, 4 blow C, 4 draw d, 5 blow E, 5 draw f♯, 6 blow G]

Whole step G-a.	Whole step a-b.	Half step b-C.	Whole Step C-d.	Whole step d-E.	Whole step E-f♯.	Half step f♯-G.
1	1	½	1	1	1	½

2nd position, *'Cross-harp'*, holes 2 to 6 is commonly used for playing blues on harmonica. With this country-tuning change, blues technique with its musical expressions, can play exact melodies and improvisations using holes 2 through 9 as well. Hole blow-9G can easily be altered by *blow-bending* on 9G down to *9F♯*, creating the upper octave of the G major scale.

As illustrated on page 11, placing a valve on hole 5 draw-reed plate, adds a blow-bend tone for more expression with this chromatic tone. Valves (wind savers) for the harmonica may be purchased online. A tiny drop of model glue will hold the valve in place.

This tuning also creates melodic possibilities in a minor key using '5th Position'. Starting on hole 5-blow for E minor, a relative minor to the Key of G, because it uses the same key signature (E to E, holes 2-blow to 5-blow then on to 8-Blow: E, f♯, G, a, b, C, d, E, f♯, G, a, b, C, d, E).

Many renowned harmonica artists have been using country-tuning for decades. Country-tuned harmonicas are readily available through most music stores or online in all 12 keys. You may tune the reed by thinning the tip of the reed, but this takes some skill. Purchasing a factory country-tuned harmonica or using a skilled musician-technician is highly recommended. A country-tuned harmonica can be used to perform jazz, gospel, country, western, folk, patriotic, classical, bluegrass and popular standards as well as blues and rock and roll. With possible chromatic capabilities, the 10-hole harmonica is a remarkable human achievement that can produce a variety of sounds using over 2½ octaves in a major or minor key.

Musical Notation and Tablature

Key to symbols:
Arrows point up for blow (exhale ↑) notes are shown in lowercase letters.
Arrows point down for draw (inhale ↓) notes are shown in lowercase letters.
Numbers are used to indicate which hole to play.
Bent arrow shafts (↳↑) indicate blow-bend or draw-bend tones.

Standard Musical notation precisely identifies the note representing the desired pitch showing melody, implying harmony and musical form. These concepts tablature alone cannot convey. I hope you enjoy learning about our ever-expanding diatonic harmonica!

Diatonic Harmonica (*Richter-tuned*)

Creative harmonica players discovered that the blues-friendly G Mixolydian mode with its lowered 7th degree could be played by starting with the draw 2 hole, the tone g in 2nd position of the harmonica. At this point, nothing had been changed in the Richter tuning system, but the importance of the cross-harp style cannot be overstated when playing blues, rock or jazz on the diatonic harmonica.

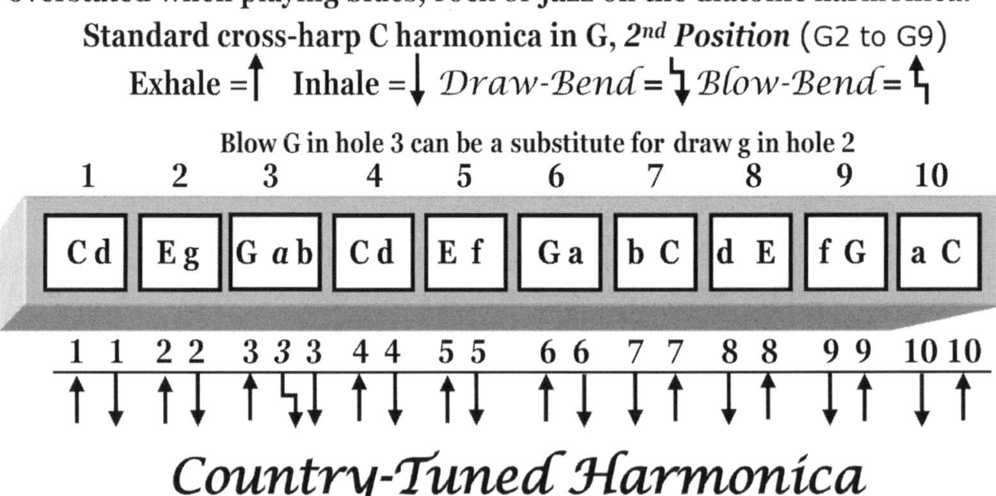

Country-Tuned Harmonica

Created on a C Harmonica in G Major with a raised f♯, hole 5 draw, 2nd position, holes 2-9.

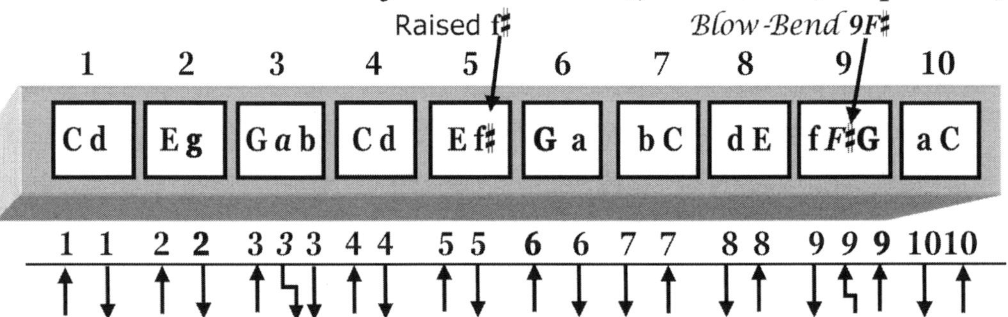

Country-Tuned Harmonica Chart

Harp Key	2nd Major
C	G
D♭	A♭
D	A
E♭	B♭
F	C
E	B
F♯	C♯
G	D
A♭	E♭
A	E
B♭	F
B	F♯

2nd Position (Major scale with the raised 7th)

All twelve keys can be country tuned by raising the 5th hole draw reed ½ step. If not, factory made, then have a harmonica technician tune it. This tuning requires a thinning of the reed tip, raising the reed-tone ½ step creating a major scale (hole-2 draw, 3-*draw bend*, 3-draw, 4-blow, 4-draw, 5-draw sharp, 6- blow). More significantly, blues harmonica players with their techniques, musical expression using improvisation can play the major scale with precise melodic pitches. Holes 6-blow to 9-blow, the upper octave, in hole-9 *blow-bend* down ½ step, creates the upper major scale.

EMBOUCHURE *(Placement of the lips on the harmonica)*

When playing the harmonica purse the lips, taller than wider to create an oval opening like whistling, around the hole to be played. Placing the harmonica inside the lips, seal the air around the hole, allowing the air to travel into a single hole.

Lips Blocking Surrounding Holes

The lips allow air into a single hole, either exhaling (blowing) or inhaling (drawing).

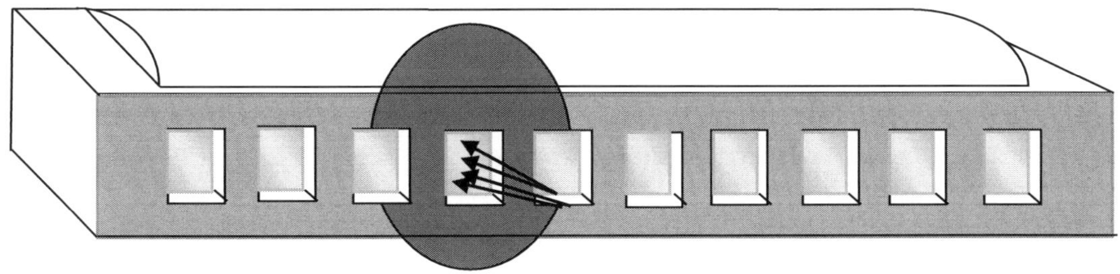

VIBRATO: Creating a Warmer Tone

(Without the traditional cupped right hand technique effect)

Continuously puffing air in or out through the harmonica creates a warm and even "vibrato". Produce a steady 4 beats, 1 puff per beat. Then 2 puffs, 4 puffs and even 8 puffs per beat; eventually an even sound will take on a life of its own and occur automatically. A long, straight (non-vibrato) tone produces a *cold*, seemingly unpleasant sound. Many players however, begin with a straight tone, then create the wavering "vibrato." Most use this method on the longer notes in the music. This technique creates a warm, desirable tone quality.

Creating the Vibrato Effect

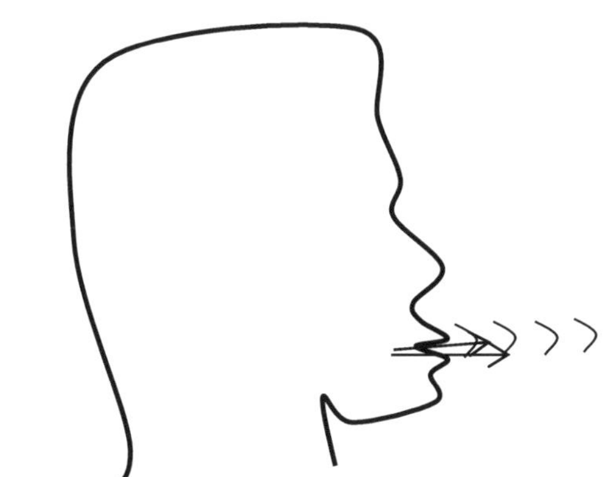

Exhaling, (blow) lightly puffing air at a steady, continuous rate.

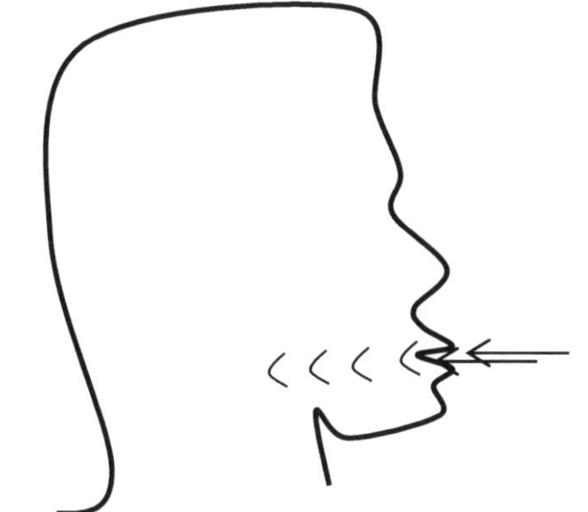

Inhale, (draw) air at a steadily continuous rate.

BENDING A PITCH LOWER (Flatting)

1) Air pressure and direction can *lower a harmonica pitch.* Draw the air to the bottom of the mouth toward the throat/lungs. This slows the reed vibrations that affect pitch. Practice and persistence are necessary to learn this skill. It is easier to bend down on a lower-pitched harmonicas in the key of 'B♭' or 'A'.

2) Draw hole 4 (*lowering* d to d♭). Next, draw hole 1 (*lowering* d to d♭), then draw 5 (*lowering* f♯ to f *natural*) & move to hole 6 (*lowering* A to A♭), repeat many times. Each hole has its challenges. I have chosen this progression pattern of holes to help achieve success.

3) First develop a solid, clear original tone in draw 3. (3 draw B *bends* to B♭, A, A♭). Draw 2G, then *bends* the tone to f *sharp* then to f *natural.* Do not add excessive air pressure to "choke/stop" the tone. Draw air gently then slightly more forcefully in a downward manner.

4) *Bend* each pitch down then release/relax the tone back to its original pitch.

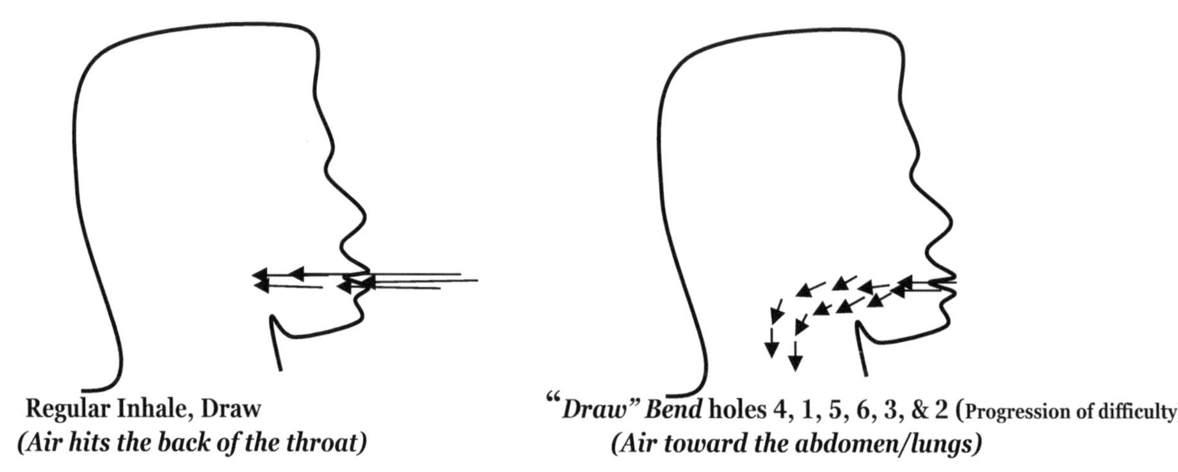

Regular Inhale, Draw
(Air hits the back of the throat)

"*Draw" Bend* holes 4, 1, 5, 6, 3, & 2 (Progression of difficulty)
(Air toward the abdomen/lungs)

"Blow-Bend" utilizes the same techniques as the draw, only reversed. Blow air, at a *downward angle*, into the reed chamber. Lower the tongue behind the bottom teeth, this creates a larger cavity that slows the air speed and *lowers the pitch* in holes 8, 9 & 10. The same thing happens when whistling.

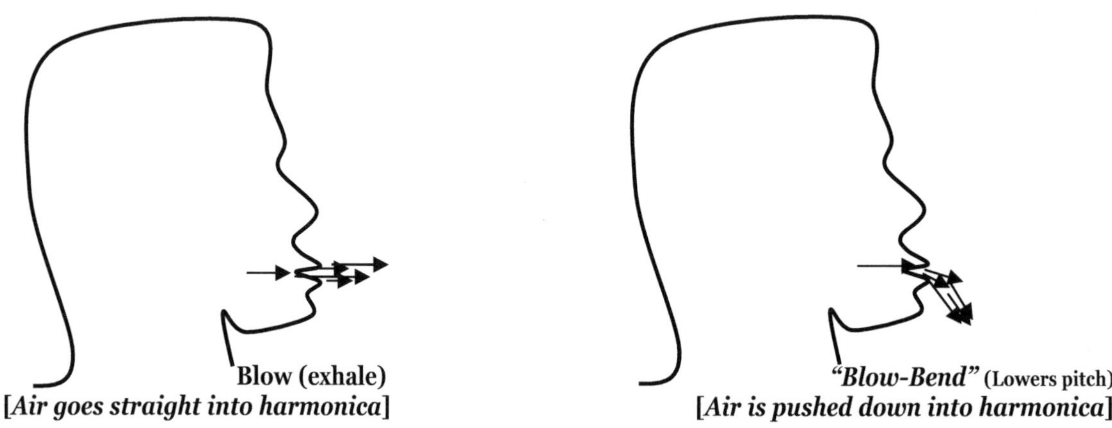

Blow (exhale)
[*Air goes straight into harmonica*]

"Blow-Bend" (Lowers pitch)
[*Air is pushed down into harmonica*]

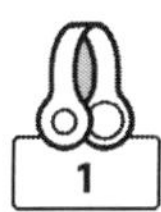

Playing a G Major Scale on the Country-Tuned C Harmonica

Draw-bending hole **5f sharp** to **5f *natural*** *is possible on the lower G scale*

Ex. A

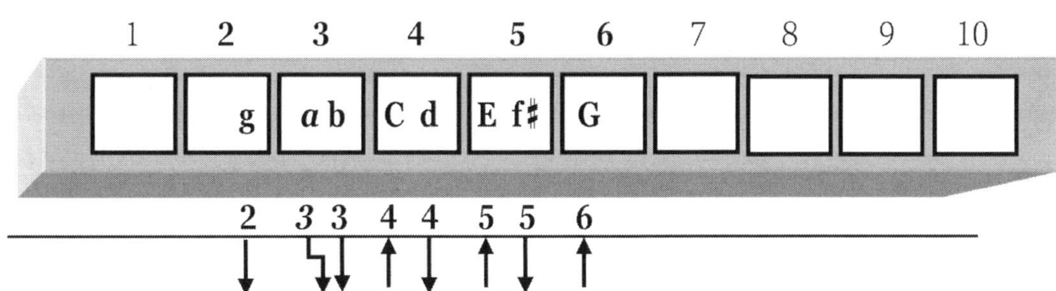

Ex. B

Without a *blow-bend*, **the upper G scale has a f natural** (mixolydian mode)

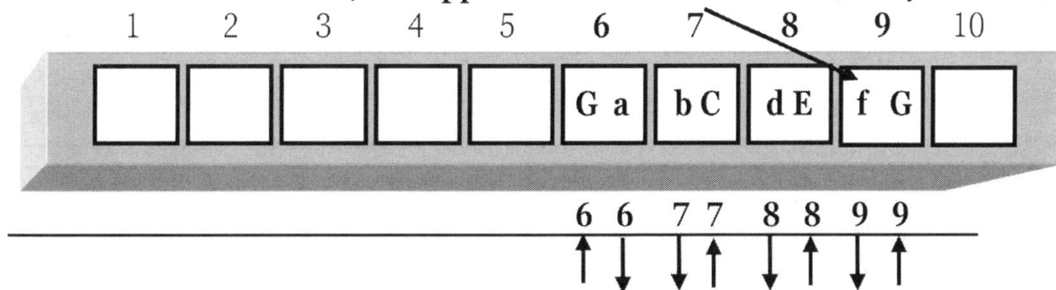

Ex. C

With a *blow-bend*, **in hole 9, two-octave G major scale is possible: Holes 2 to 9**

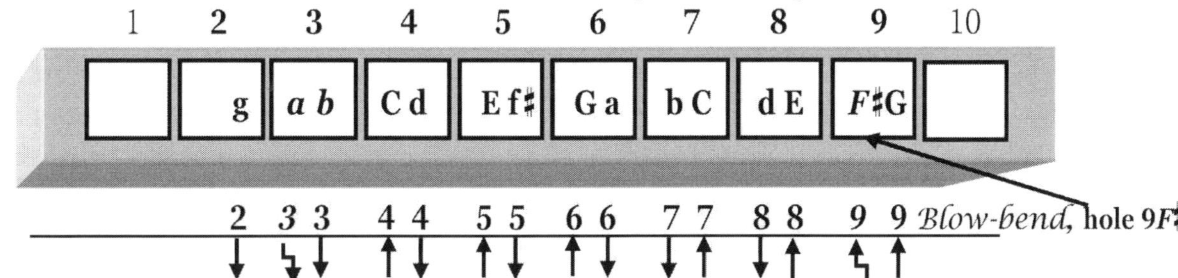

Ex. D

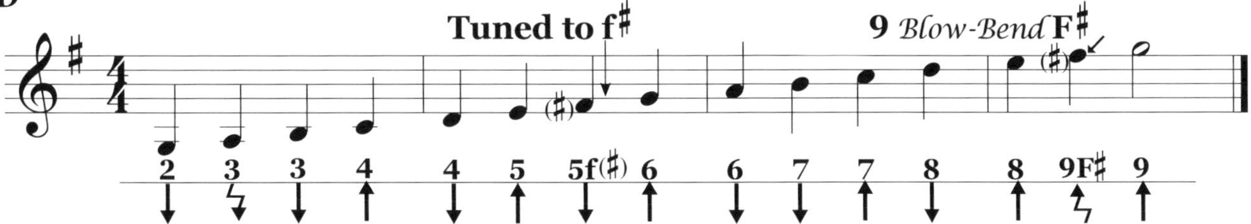

Ex. E

Added notes above and below in holes 1, 2 (C, d, E) **& 10 (a, C)**

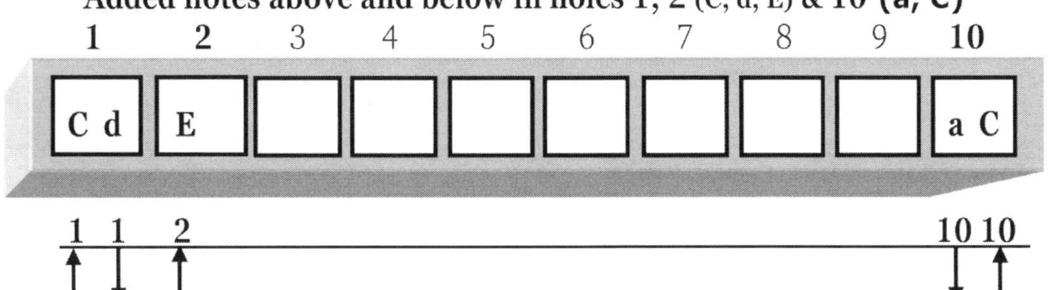

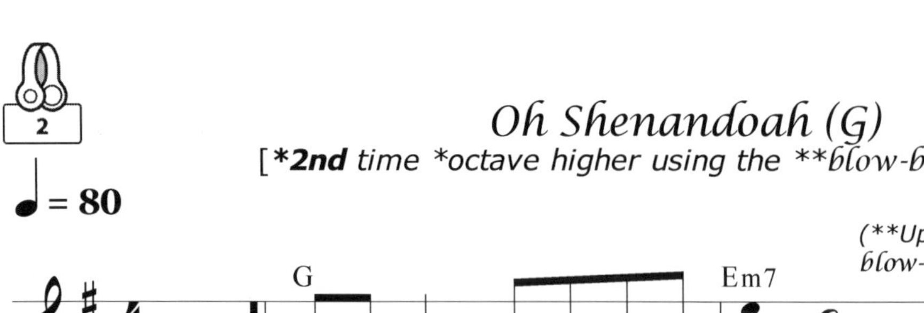

Oh Shenandoah (G)

[*2nd time *octave higher using the **blow-bend F♯, hole 9]

Traditional

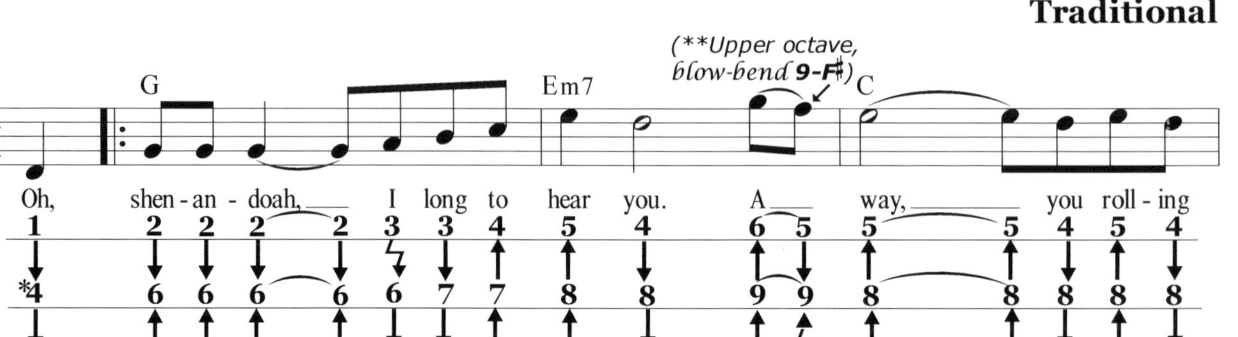

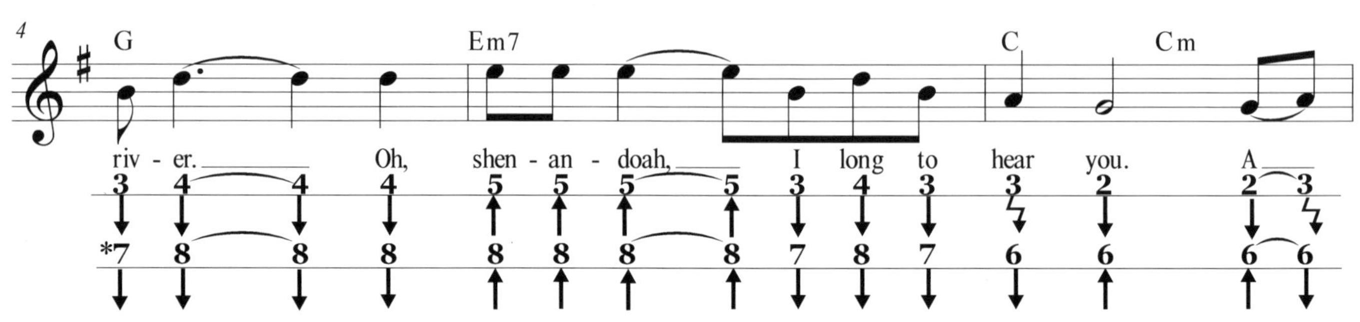

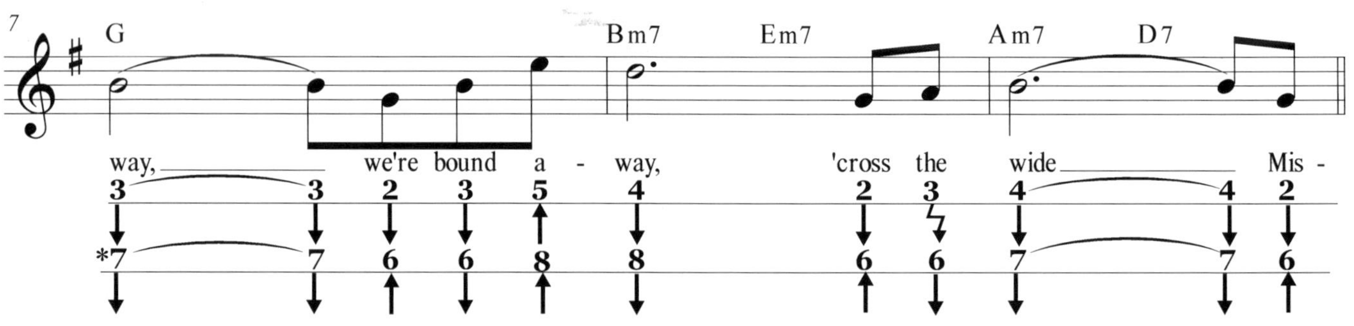

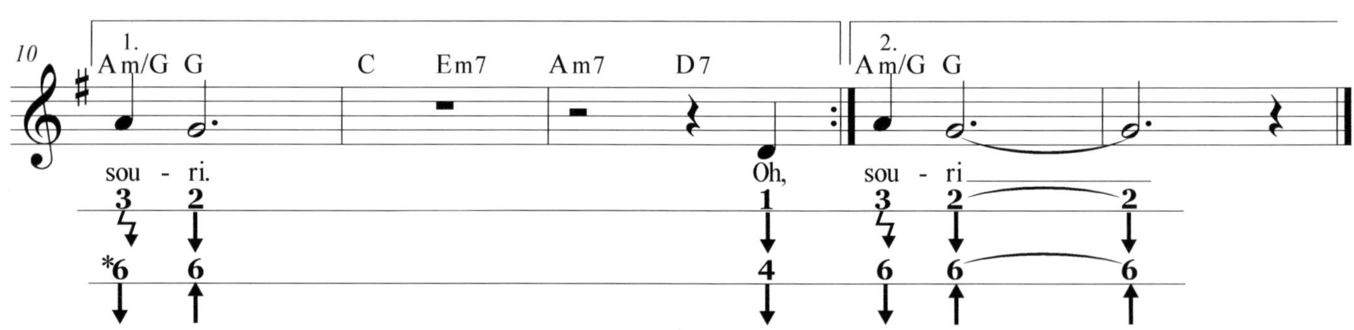

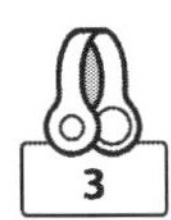

Silent Night (G)

[***2nd** time, *Partially play an octave higher, starting on hole **8**]

Franz Gruber

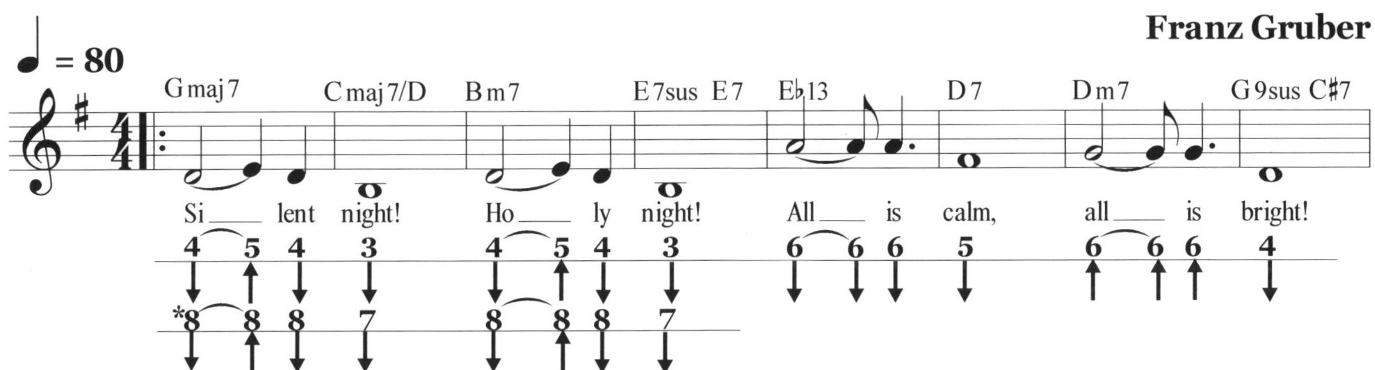

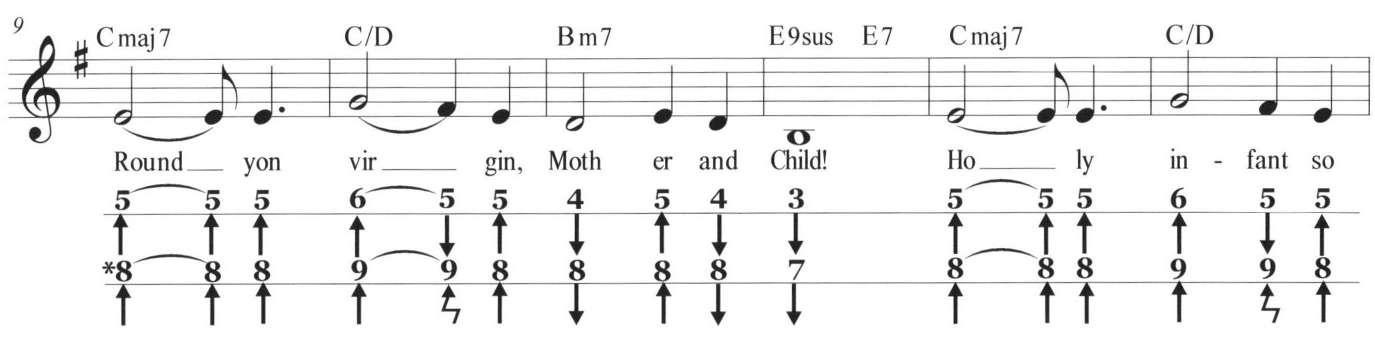

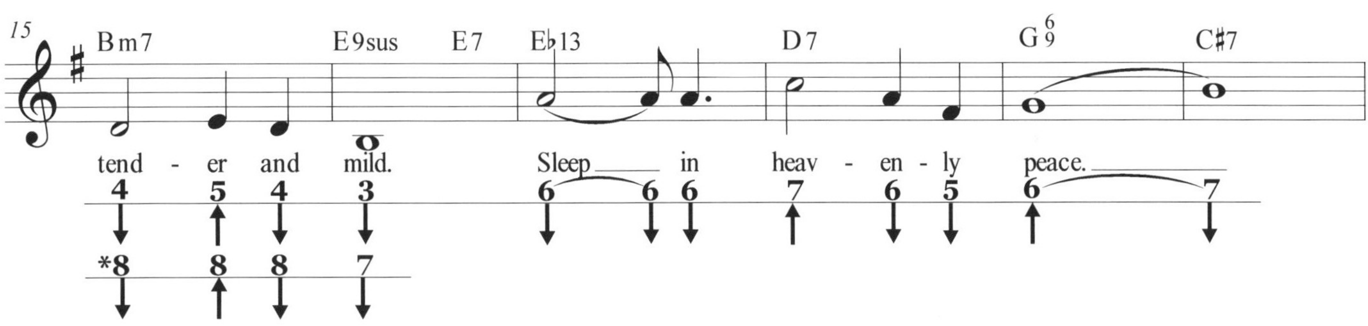

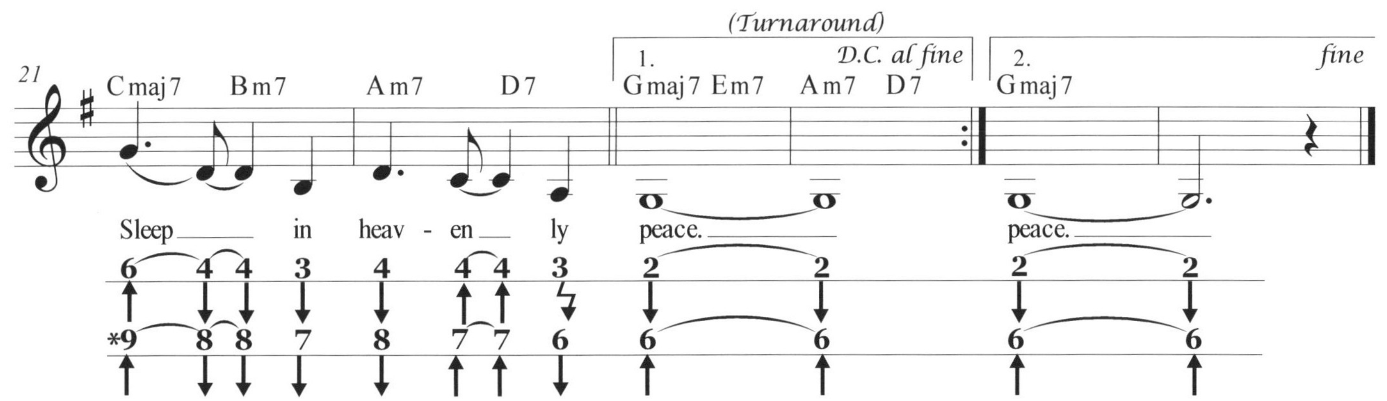

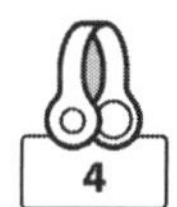

The Sloop John B. (G)

[***2nd** time play one octave lower starting on hole **1**]

♩ = 105

Traditional Folk-Country

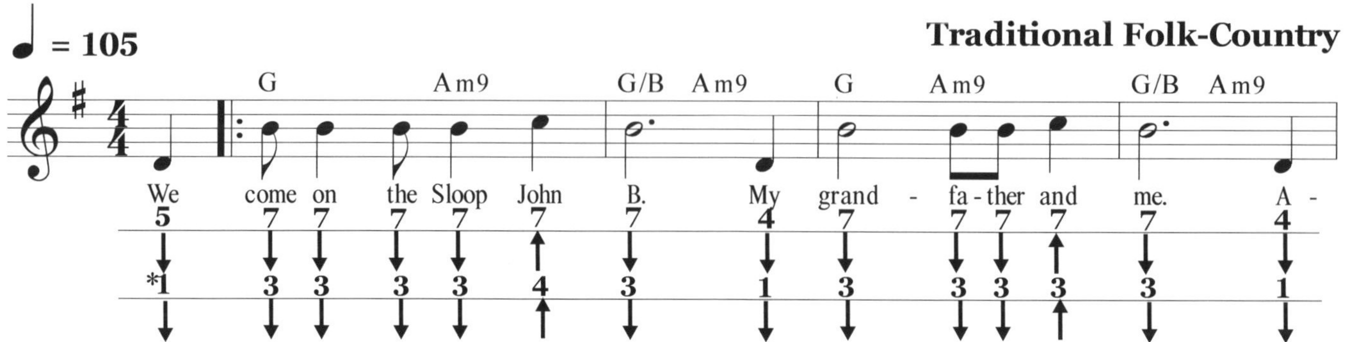

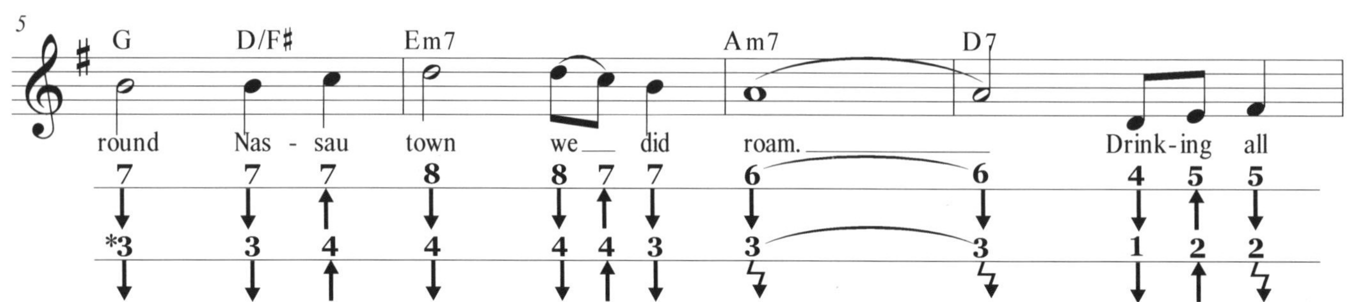

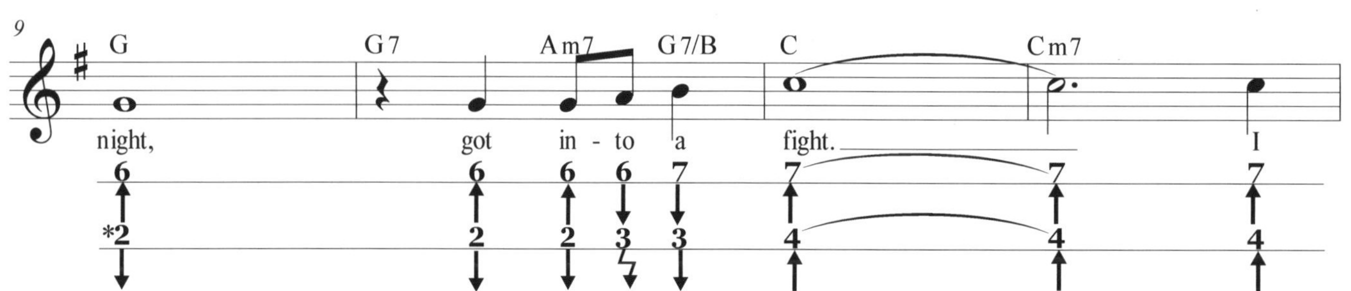

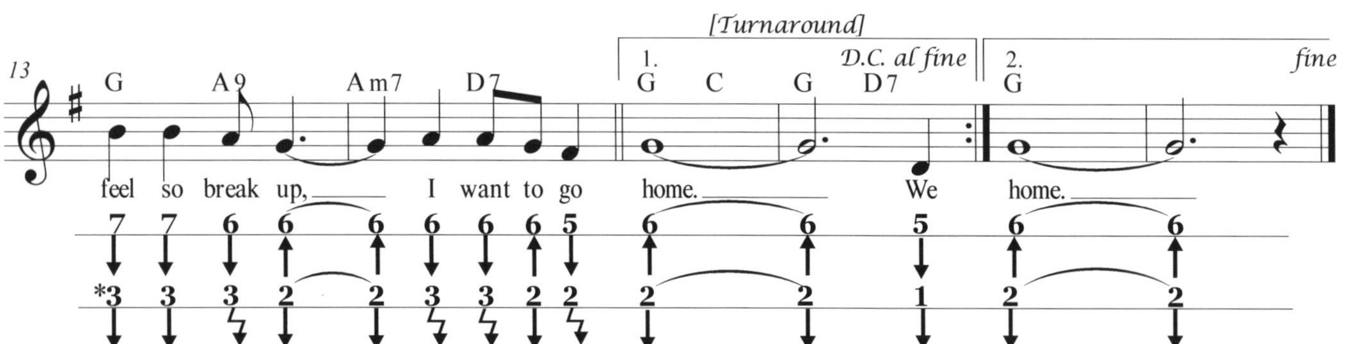

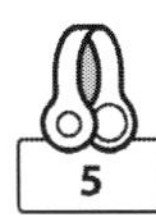

ANOTHER HARMONICA ADJUSTMENT

With tuning and placing a valve on hole 5, it is recommended you look at the *Harmonicare Chart for Chromatic and Diatonic Harmonica* (MB94752) by Phil Duncan.

Placing a valve (wind saver) over the 5th hole, draw reed

Tools: *Small Phillip's screw driver, scissors, model glue, valve (It is best to practice on an old draw reed plate.)*

1) *Remove all the screws, disassembling the harmonica.*
2) *Lay the valve next to the reed slot (The draw reed plate has descending rivets.)*
3) *Cut the length of the valve to fit over the rivet to the end of the reed slot.*
4) *Glue the valve on top of the 5th slot, at the rivet, (careful No glue on the reed), then center the (plastic) valve.*
5) *Use the comb to check the valve position. The valve should not touch the comb! Let it dry completely!*
6) *Reassemble the harmonica.*

A tiny drop of model glue goes on under the valve tip only.

Draw Reed Plate *(descending rivets)*

The valve shuts off the air to the draw reed allowing air pressure to *lower the blow pitch.*

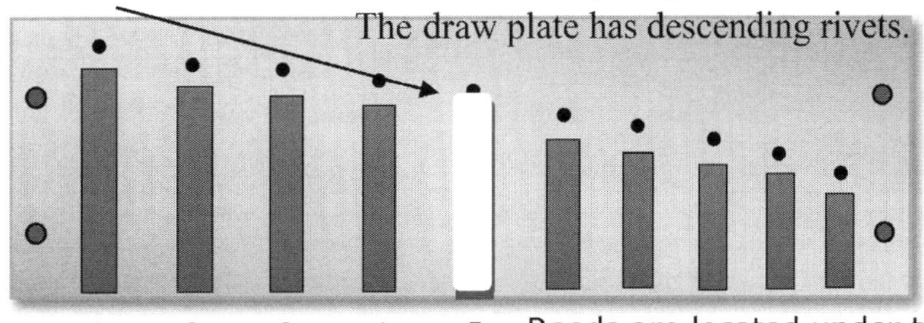

1 2 3 4 5 Reeds are located under the plate.

Valves (*sometimes known as a wind saver*) can be ordered online!
Also, check YouTube for instructional videos on how to install them.

BLOW-BEND HOLE 5 (Valve Use: Blow-Bend 'E' to 'E♭')

Reverse technique: ***Blow-bend*** **then release the air pressure for E: 'D♯' to 'E'. With the valve installed *there are now 4 chromatic* ½ steps available in hole 5: *D♯*, E, *f*, f♯ or f♯, *f*, E and *E♭*!**

Blow G, hole 3 is available, but draw 2 is preferred. *Draw-bend*, hole *5* plays *f* natural.

Ex. F

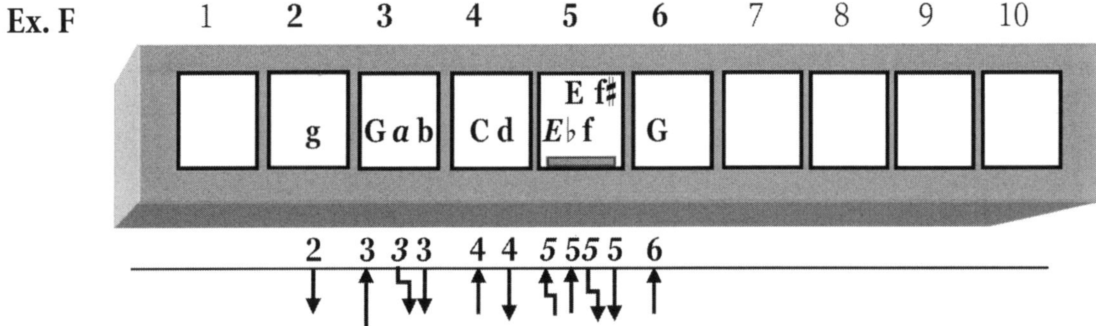

Ex. G **The valve and tuning change on the country tuned harmonica creates 4 chromatic tones in hole 5.** **D♯ and E♭ is an enharmonic (same) pitch.**

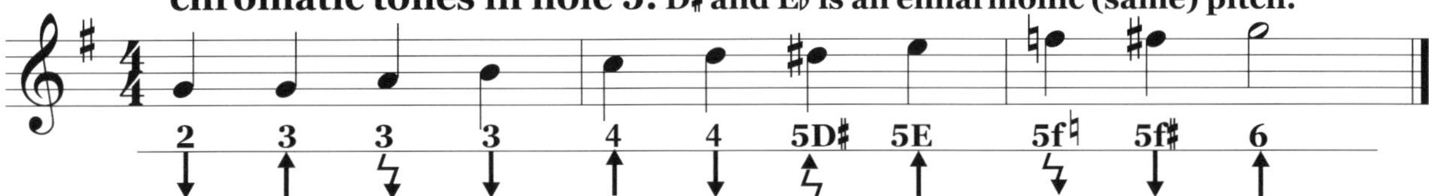

You may experiment in hole 2 *blow-bend* with a valve on the draw reed for possibilities.

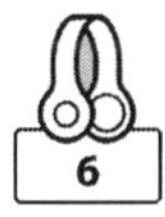

PLAYING MINOR SCALES ON THE COUNTRY-TUNED HARMONICA

On the C Richter tuned harmonica, 1st position is a Greek *Ionian* scale from hole 4-blow to 7-blow, C to C, is a major scale. 2nd position is a Greek *Mixolydian* scale with a flat 7th, G to G, hole 2-draw to 6-blow. 3rd position is a *Dorian* scale, D to D, hole 4-draw to 8-draw. 4th Position is an *Aeolian* scale, ***a natural minor scale,*** A to A, hole 3 *bend-draw* to 6-draw a ***relative minor*** to C major. The 5th position is a ***Phrygian*** scale E to E, hole 5-blow to 8-blow. Each *modal* scale has a different whole and half step arrangement. Each note of the major scale, serves as the first note or tonic of each 7-note *modal* scale.

With the altered hole-5 reed (f to f♯ on country tuned C diatonic harmonica) gives the ability to play a complete G *major* scale along with its relative E *natural/harmonic minor* scale. The keys of G major and E minor are "relative" or related by sharing the same key signature. Having installed the valve (wind saver) in hole 5, adds the major 7th *blow-bend* tone below the E tonic in hole 5. If you play the song "Georgia on My Mind" in G major, 2nd position, the bridge or 'B' section, is in E minor, or 5th position, the relative minor of G major, 2nd position.

Country-Tuned Harmonica Chart for major and minor scales

There are three minor scales:

1. **Natural or pure minor:** [E, f♯, G, a, b, C, d, E];
2. **Harmonic minor:** [E, f♯, G, a, b, C, D♯, E];
3. **Melodic minor:** 6th and 7th degree are raised a half tone on the ascent and lowered (reverting) to pure minor on the descent. (not commonly used)

Harp Key	2nd Major	5th Minor
C	G	Em
D♭	A♭	Fm
D	A	F♯m
E♭	B♭	Gm
E	B	A♭m
F	C	Am
F♯	C♯	B♭m
G	D	Bm
A♭	E♭	Cm
A	E	D♭m
B♭	F	Dm
B	F♯	E♭m

Note:
Natural minor does not use the valve in hole 5.

Note:
It is called D♯ when moving up the scale.
It is called E♭ when going down the scale.

Upper natural/harmonic minor scales, 5th *position* (E5 blow to E8 blow)
D♯/E♭ *blow-bend* creates Harmonic Minor/Draw d, hole 8 is plays natural minor.

Ex. H

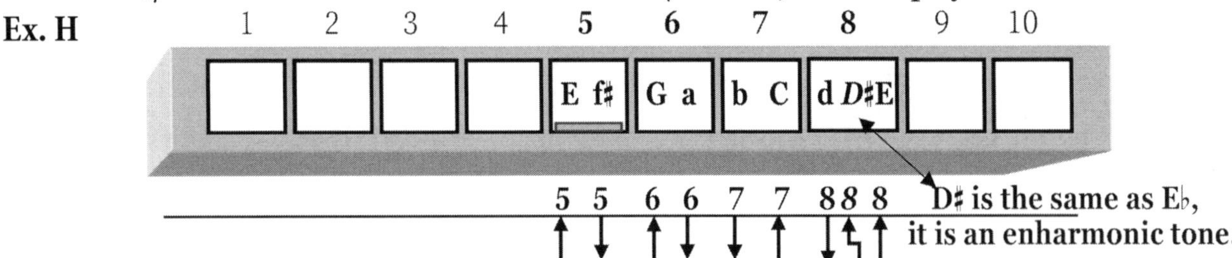

Ex. I

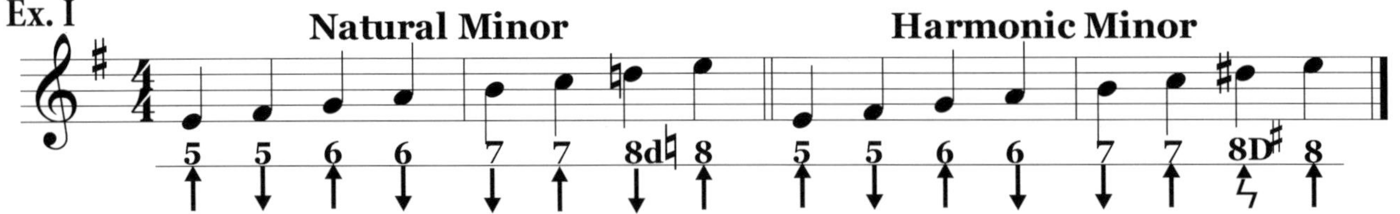

Ex. J **Lower Harmonic Minor Scale, *5th Position*** **(E to E, holes 2 to 5)**

D♯/E♭ *bend-blow* note for harmonic minor scale

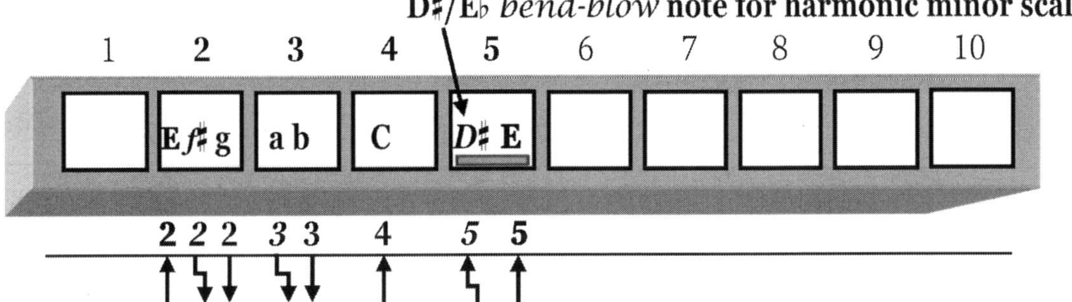

Ex. K **Two-Octaves Harmonic Minor Scales, *5th Position*** **(E to E)**

Harmonic minor allows soloing over the major dominant chord (such as B7)

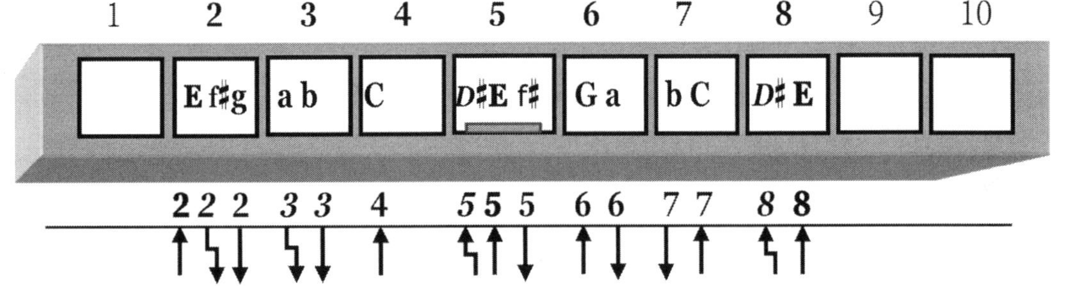

Ex. L **Notation of the E Harmonic Minor Scale, Ascending (*D♯*) and Descending (*E♭*)**

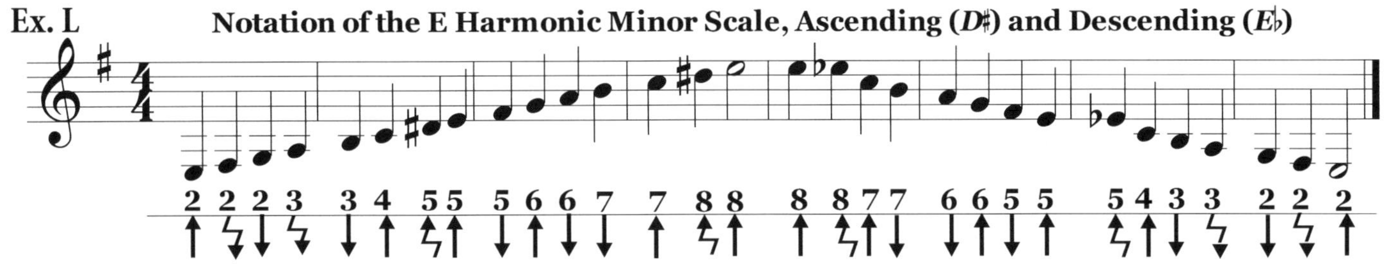

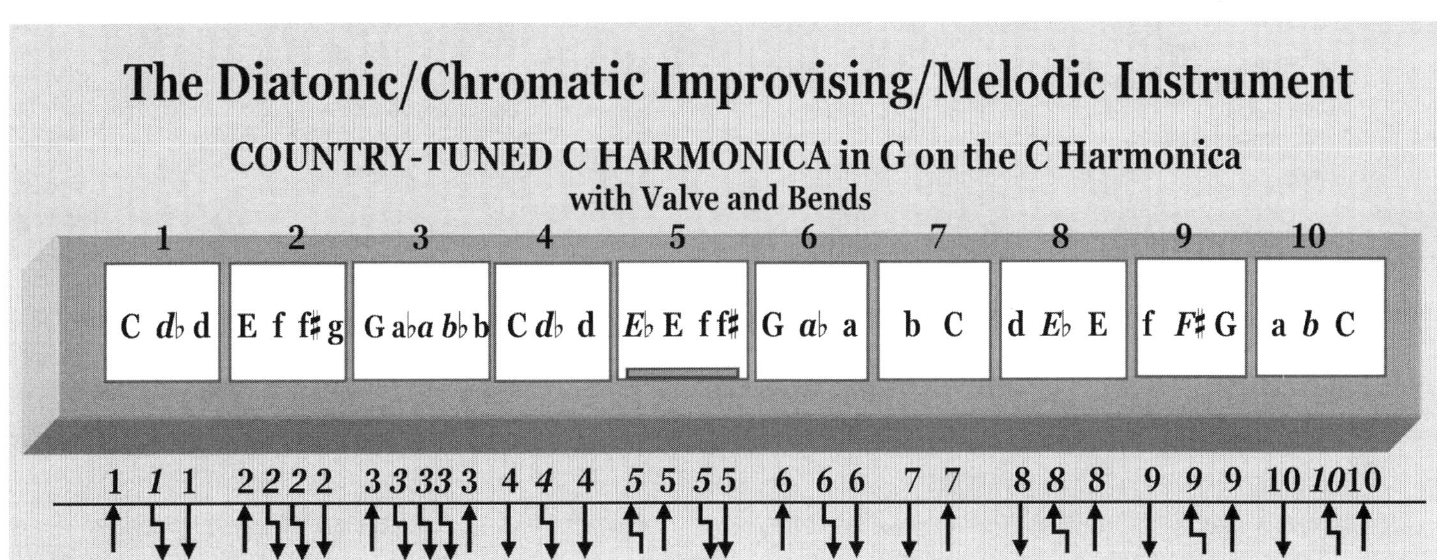

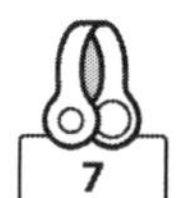

Poor Wayfaring Stranger (Em) [*NoValve*]

[***2nd** time one Octave lower. **E** in hole **2**]

5th Position *(E Natural Minor)* **Traditional Folk**

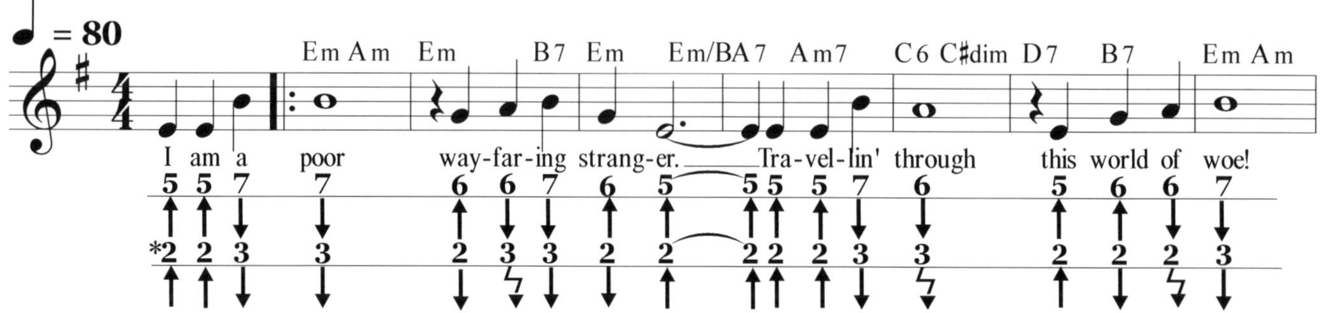

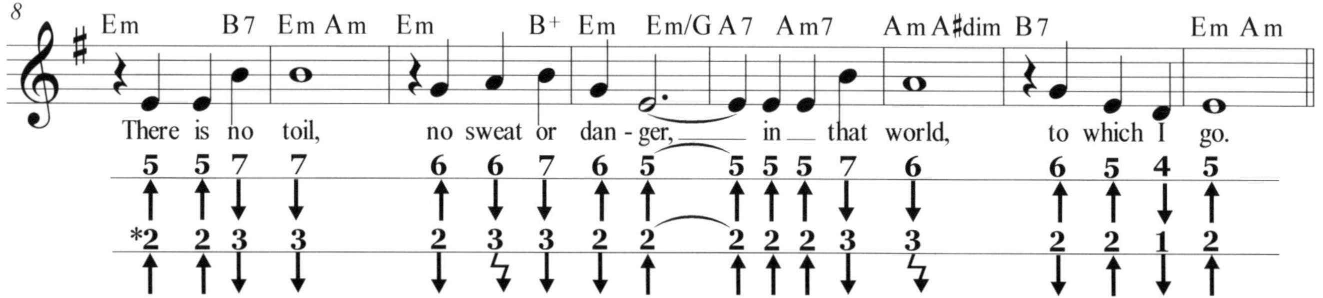

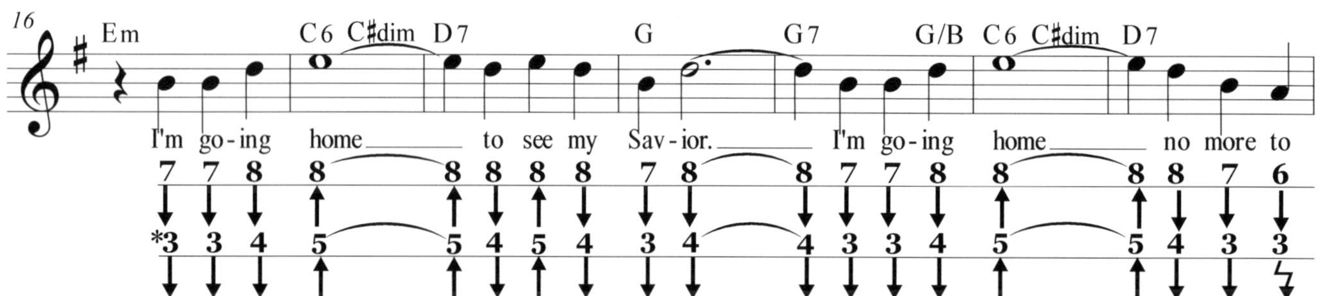

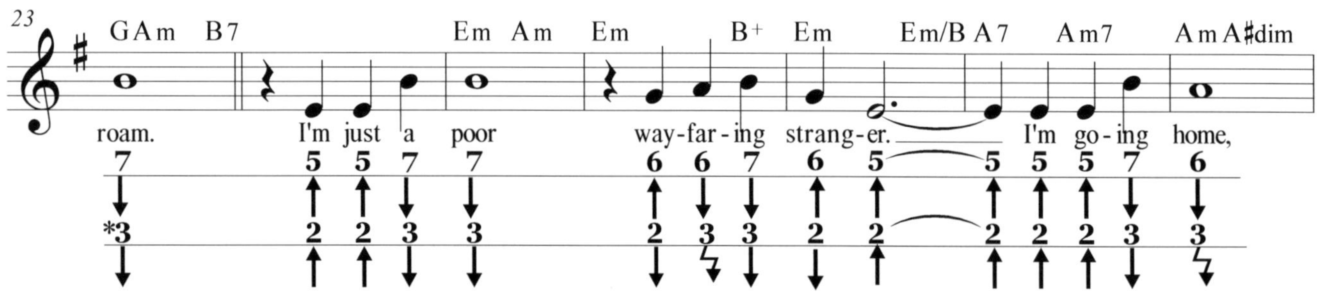

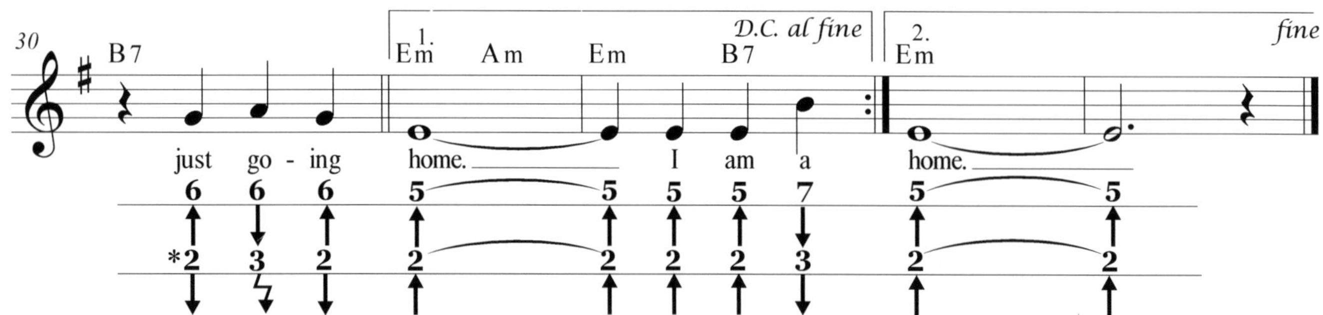

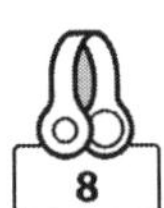

St. James Infirmary (Em) *[No Valve]*

[***2nd** time, play one (1) octave lower starting on blow **E**, hole **2**]

5th Position *(E Minor)*

Traditional Folk

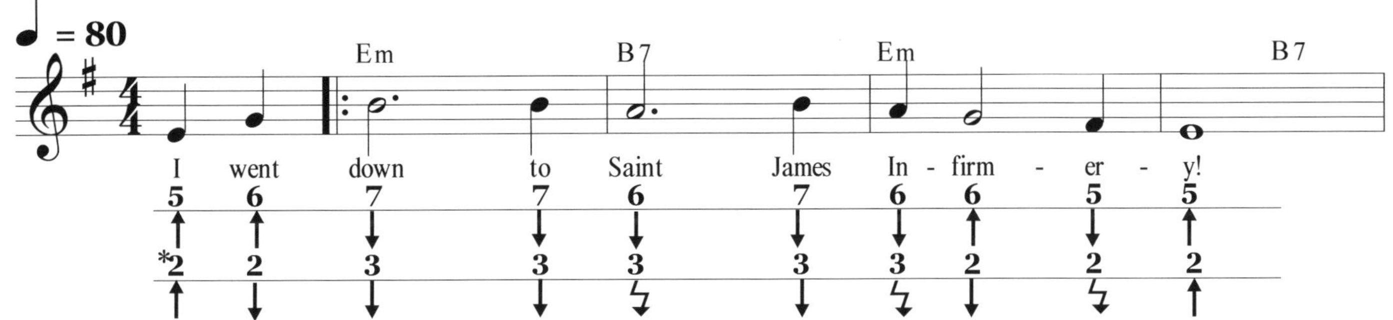

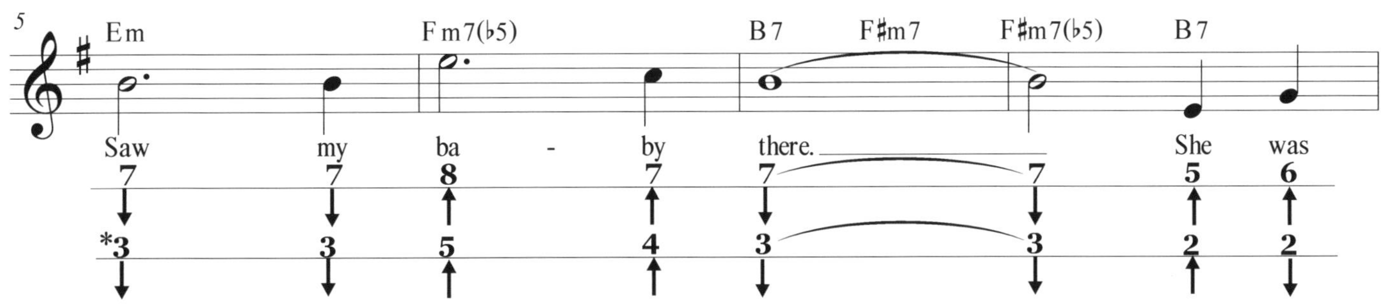

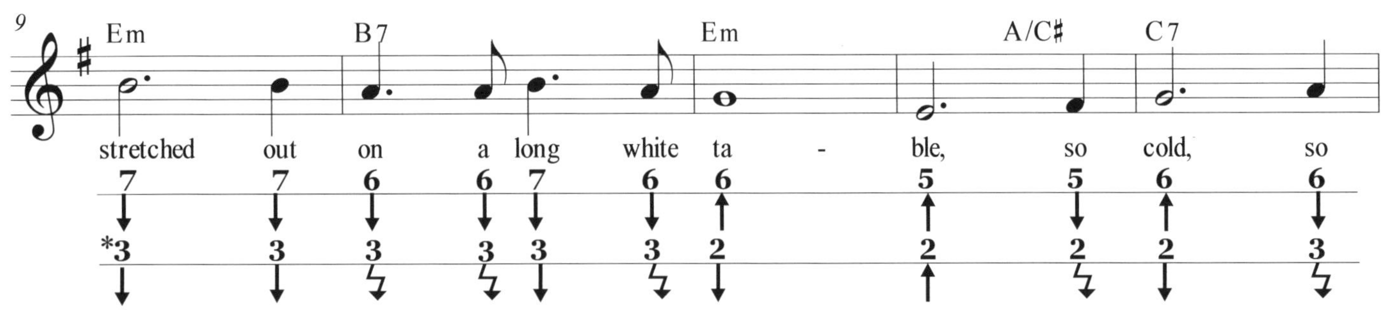

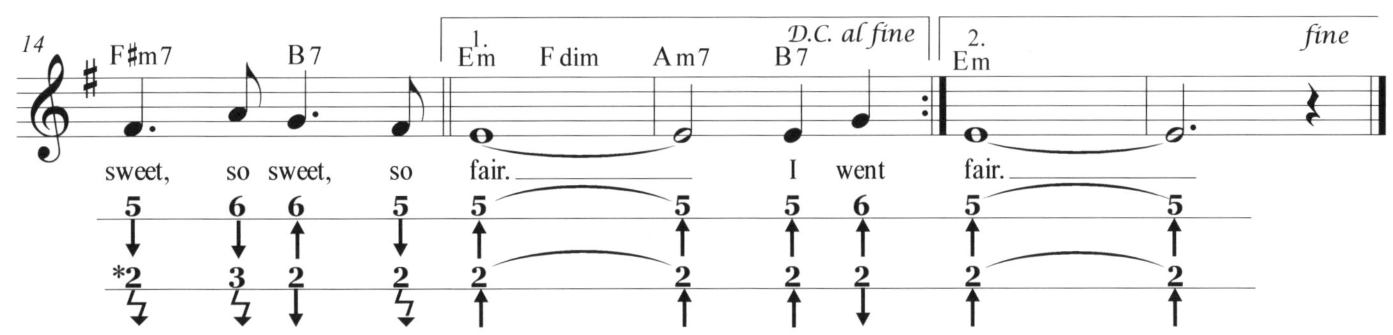

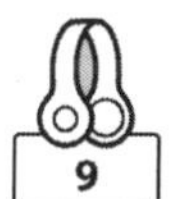

Joshua Fit the Battle of Jericho (Em)

[*Blow-bend* on hole **5** using the valve]

5th Position (*E Harmonic Minor*) **Traditional**

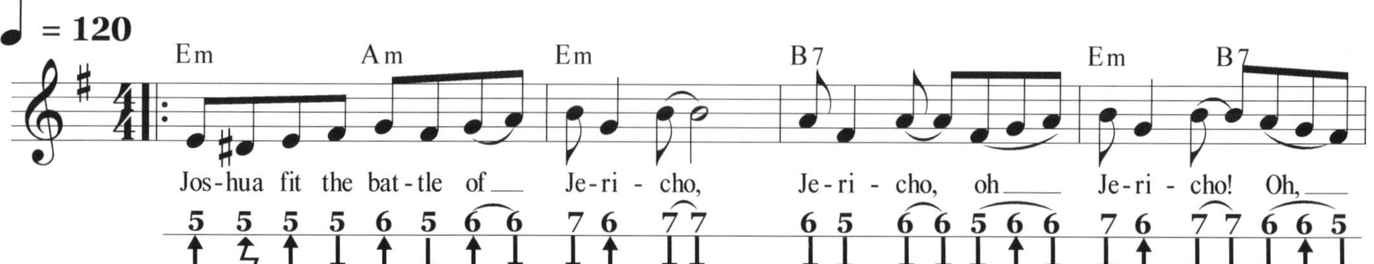

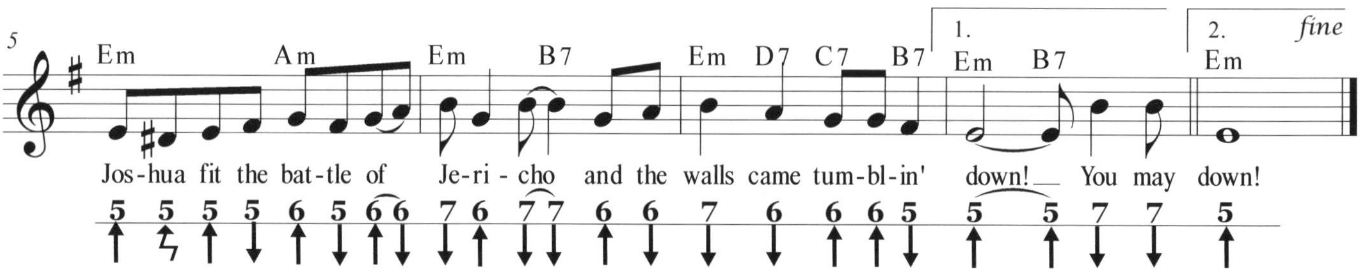

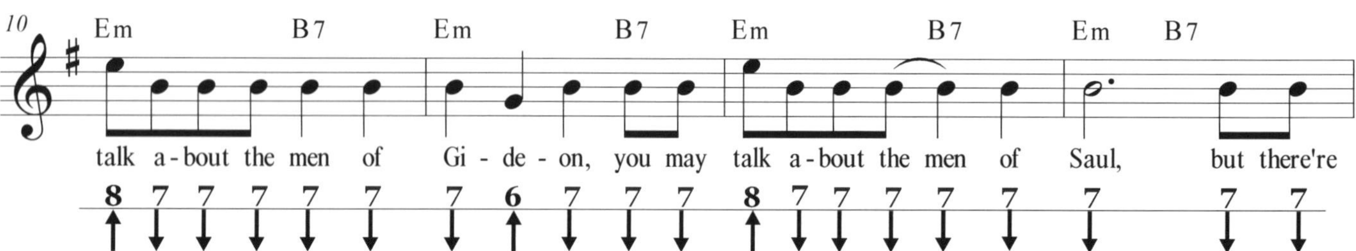

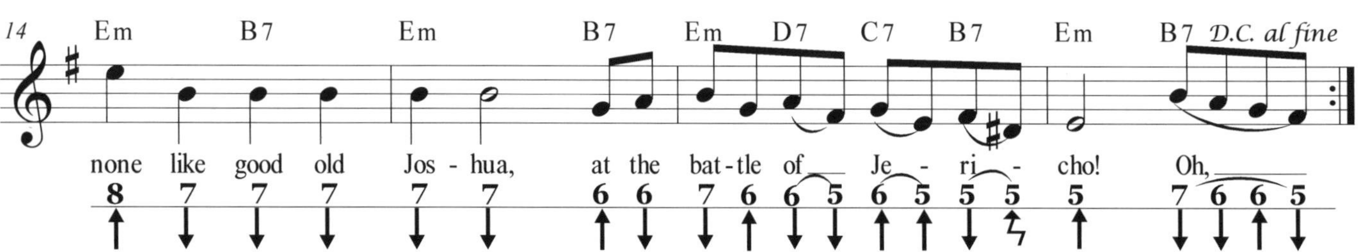

In Summary, the standard Richter tuned C diatonic harmonica can play a G mixolydian scale with a flat 7th starting with the G tone, hole 2-draw, and play to the next G tone. Tuning the 5th hole reed by raising the 5-draw reed ½ step, forms the G major scale with the major 7th f♯ tone. Yet, we can physically lower, *draw-bend*, the raised 7th tone hole 5-draw to f-natural. Both notes are available. The valve placed over the 5th hole draw reed creates the major 7th tone for the E minor harmonic scale in 5th position. These changes enhance the versatility of the 10-hole diatonic harmonica for 2nd and 5th positions. There may be other innovations. Time will tell!